Courageous Inspirations

Keys to Unlock Life's Blessings

By

Doyvon Montgomery

ISBN: 978-969-2292-61-0

DEDICATION

In Loving Memory of my Granny, Mother Doris Mae Humphrey Bryant. Her life and the words she spoke in my life when I was a young girl came to pass and are my inspiration.

In Loving Memory of my grandfather, Pop, William Montgomery, Sr. His inspiration of love and family will always remain with me.

KEYS TO A SPIRITUAL LIFE

FOREWORD BY
JC GARDNER

Beloved Reader:

Get ready to be inspired and transformed. What you are about to read are spiritual keys to not only unlock life's blessings, but these keys will open doors to your heart and will reveal God's presence in your life.

Have you ever been to church and the pastor's sermon seems like it was written specifically for you? It's like he/she knew just what you were going through and once the sermon was finished, you felt redeemed because God found a way to get your attention. Through that vessel, He let you know, "I got you. You are not alone. I feel your pain. I know your situation." The word preached that day fueled your journey, allowing you to go on.

God uses people all the time to deliver messages. He meets us where we're at. Through Courageous Inspirations, Doyvon has allowed God's grace and wisdom to speak to people from all walks of life. She leaves no stone unturned in her quest to enlighten and save as many souls as possible through practical examples and scriptural references. Courageous Inspirations provides real-life illustrations of how one can truly live a Spirit-filled life. Doyvon's anointing is unmistakable, as her style comes through as authentic and nonjudgmental, teaching and guiding us back to the one who loves us unconditionally, forgives our sins, and grants us peace that surpasses all understanding, Christ Jesus.

Before you embark on this life-changing journey, grab a journal or highlighter, as there are many gems of wisdom you won't want to forget. Even for those who are well-versed with biblical principles, there are new discoveries for everyone.

Dare to be courageous! Wake up every day inspired. No matter your circumstances or where you are in your spiritual walk, never forget there's a place for you in God's kingdom. May God's grace and mercy bless and keep you today and always.

JC Gardner is an award-winning author, ghostwriter, writing coach, and speaker. Helping new and aspiring authors bring their stories to life through her coaching program is a blessing and a gift. She enjoys speaking life into women who have forsaken their gifts and talents and encourages them to walk boldly into their destiny.

www.jc-gardner.com

INTRODUCTION BY DOYVON MONTGOMERY

All scripture was taken from the King James Version of the Bible.

I am so happy you picked up this book. I pray you are inspired to grow deeper in your relationship with the Lord. In this spiritual growth book, you will learn about keys to receive blessings, freedom, healing, and many other benefits from God. You will be equipped with knowledge to invite God into your home, family, relationships, church, and personal life.

This book is a compilation of some of the Christian blogs that I have written since 2014. I wrote Courageous Inspirations because I am passionate about sharing the word of God and the impact it has had on my life. I received miracles, deliverance, transformation, empowerment, and many awesome experiences because of applying biblical principles. My passion is to encourage others to apply the Word of God so that they can experience the Lord in a special way too.

May God bless you as you read this book.

1
BE BLESSED

"The Lord bless thee, and keep thee: The Lord make his face shine upon thee, and be gracious unto thee: The Lord lift up his countenance upon thee, and give the peace." – Numbers 6:24-26

THE KEY TO BEING BLESSED

The key to being blessed is how you receive and obey the word of God. Many people use the word blessed but may not experience the blessings from the Lord. There are many definitions and words to describe blessed such as: favored, fortunate, bringing happiness and thankfulness, glad, merry, heartening, joyful, holy, sacred, divine, adored, sanctified, and enjoying the bliss of heaven. God wants to release these words and every blessing in our life.

In the Bible, there are many verses that say "Blessed are they" followed by instructions to receive the blessing. Revelation 1:3 notes you are blessed if you read, hear, and keep the Word of God. If you rarely read your Bible and you are not giving your best effort to live by it, then unfortunately you are hindering the flow of your blessings. It is important to include Bible reading in our lives, not just when we attend church, but in our personal time as well. Reading the Bible, obeying, and living it ties in with our blessings.

God wants to bless, speak to you, and transform your life through His Word. Psalm 1 encourages us to not seek ungodly counsel but seek counsel and direction from His Word. We will be blessed and whatever we do will prosper if we meditate on the word of God day and night (Psalm 1:1-3). To be blessed is to not walk in the path of sinners. You are blessed when you live a life that is pleasing and holy to God. Does your circle encourage you to be godly? Or do they pump you up to sin and allow you to stay in that comfort zone? It is important to be around people that will help you to be blessed by becoming that tree that will bear fruit in the Lord. Surround yourself with godly people that will help you to grow and draw closer to God and not further from Him.

Money and physical things do not mean you are blessed by God. You can have wealth, nice cars, a beautiful home, prosperous career, and still not have a relationship with the Lord. You can be rich on this earth, which is great. But do not leave God out of your life. You do not want to have earthly things only and miss being blessed in your Spirit by God (Mark 8:36). In the end, all your hard work to be prosperous on earth will be a waste if you did not have Jesus too. There is nothing wrong with desiring and striving for increase. But do not stress out or let that be your only focus in life because sometimes riches can do more harm than good. It seems like people who have riches and material things would be happy. But some rich people still commit suicide. Or they get involved in drug and substance abuse to deal with their pain. Therefore, God may not allow everyone to travel the road to riches. But if we aim to be faithful to the Lord, He promises to bless us abundantly according to His will. You may not be led to millions, but you will have the blessings and the peace of God.

If you are faithful to God, you will abound with blessings (Proverbs 28:20). When you are faithful, you do not stop. You do not take extended breaks or pause when you don't feel like it or things aren't going your way. You stay faithful no matter what. That is the faithfulness God is looking for. Some people only deal with God for the month of January for a New Year's resolution and December when they feel good for the holidays. However, God is looking for vessels who will love and walk with Him daily, monthly, and year after year. Faithful servants of God can expect blessings from Heaven (Deuteronomy 28:1-8).

BLESSINGS COME IN UNEXPECTED PACKAGES

May God sharpen our spiritual radar and equip us to follow His Spirit to recognize His ordained blessings that are wrapped in unexpected packages. May our hearts be conditioned, opened and ready to accept the unusual wrapping and packages of our blessings. God knows the inside scoop of every blessing even if it does not make sense to us. It is important to trust that He will lead us to blessings that may not look the best outwardly but are good because God already knows the quality, potential, and the things that will bloom in time. The stories in the Bible inspired me to change my limited view of how I want blessings to be packaged.

Like Samuel in 1 Samuel 16:7, we can think a person, place, or thing is the blessing because of the outer appearance. We look at the outer appearance, but God looks at the heart. It can look good, but is it really good inside? God told Samuel the blessing was in the house of a man named Jesse, but He didn't tell him beforehand which son to anoint to be the next king. When Samuel saw Jesse's sons, he said "surely" the oldest son is God's anointed to be the next king. And God said no he is not. Do not look at physical appearances, age, material, and outer things.

Like Samuel, we can select something just by looking at the outer package and assume it is the blessing because of how it looks. Samuel went through all of the seven sons twice that were present in the house and still didn't receive God's approval. He didn't stop looking until He found the blessing of the Lord.

Sometimes you can have many choices in front of you but those still aren't the ordained blessings. The blessing wasn't even in the house at the "moment" and, therefore, he couldn't physically see him, but He knew God told him he was a part of Jesse's family. He finally asked Jesse does he have any more kids because the ones in front of him weren't who God ordained to be king. The blessing, David, was outside working hard taking care of the sheep. God chose the youngest son who wasn't with the rest of his family at that time. He was not with the crowd. He was the reject. Always be mindful of how we treat people who are considered rejects because most times they are actually hidden jewels.

God sometimes uses unexpected people and situations to show His power and glory. Therefore, be very careful who you disqualify or put down because of their outward or current situation. God takes the ashes (the remains of things that are destroyed, useless and dead) and beautifies it! God can beautify anybody and their situation. Do not be discouraged if you are in an ugly situation right now. God specializes in turning things around into a blessing if you get in Him.

Always pray, obey, and follow God when he puts in your heart to pursue something. Whatever God leads you to will bloom into greater blessings. Follow the leading of the Lord especially when it comes to people and connections. For example, in Acts Chapter 9, Ananias did not want to go and pray for Saul because he heard about Saul's bad reputation of having Christians killed. God had to deal with his servant Ananias and tell him yes, Saul has a reputation, but He is chosen and to go pray and anoint him anyway. And look at how Paul became a mighty vessel because God told his servant to not look at his past but to still go pray and anoint him! We are still experiencing the blessings of Paul's beautiful transformation to Christ and Ananias' obedience to God. Because of Ananias' willingness to follow God and go pray for a blessing that was wrapped in an unexpected package, Paul wrote most of the New Testament Bible books that we still read today.

2
FREEDOM IN CHRIST

"If the Son therefore shall make you free, ye shall be free indeed."

- John 8:36

GET READY TO BE SET FREE

God wants to release every shackle in your life. In Acts 16:23-26, God miraculously set Paul and Silas free from prison. These servants of God were arrested and jailed for preaching the Word of God. Nevertheless, even while in prison, they prayed and worshipped God. Paul and Silas did not allow their physical chains to silence or stop the work of God in their life. They were loud enough in the jail cell that even the inmates listened to their prayers and praises at midnight. And suddenly an earthquake occurred and shook the prison's foundation. All prison doors and everyone's handcuffs were loosed. God could have only set Paul and Silas free. But because the inmates listened to the prayers and praises, they were set free too.

It is so important to get more in the presence of prayer, worship, and the word of God. Be ready to be set free as you draw closer to the things of God. God is going to touch you. The more you are in the presence of God and surrounded by people who are on fire for the Lord, you are preparing the way for chains to be broken in your life just like the inmates who listened to Paul and Silas in prison. The presence of God breaks chains.

I encourage those who send out prayers, praises, and the Word of God to continue because it creates an atmosphere for others to be set free. God wants yielded vessels like Paul and Silas who will faithfully release the Spirit of God wherever they go so that others who are around and listening will experience freedom too. Where the Spirit of the Lord is there is liberty (2 Corinthians 3:17). Therefore, do not limit your declarations about the Lord to just in your home or church. Send it out everywhere and God will do the rest.

When you invite the Spirit of God into your life, no matter what has been binding you...freedom will take place. The Spirit of God is more powerful than anything. God's Spirit broke the prison chains off Paul and Silas and the prisoner. God does not need man's key. His Spirit can immediately break any and all chains. Therefore, we need God's Spirit. Pray to receive the Holy Spirit. Do things that will invite Him in such as reading the Bible, listening to spiritual messages, praying, and worshipping.

God does not want us to quench the Spirit, which is what frees us (1 Thessalonians 5:19). The Spirit of God wants to be present in our lives, but sometimes our environments and actions are not welcoming for the Spirit. God's Spirit is Holy and is all about actions that please God. If we constantly do things that are not of God, we are quenching the Spirit and we will be bound up.

Sometimes situations arise that may bind us up and disturb our freedom. But, if we walk in the Spirit and stay obedient to God, we will not stay bound for long. In Judges Chapter 14 and 15, the Spirit of God was so strong in Samson's life that he received the strength needed to destroy a lion that came against him. When the Spirit of God came upon Samson, he broke through cords and bands on his arms and hands that were placed on him by his enemies. Samson was powerful and strong in the Lord until he disobeyed God. Disobedience caused him to no longer possess power. When his enemies bound him at the end of his life, he could not break free anymore because the Lord departed from him.

I pray that God will set you free in Jesus' name. Amen.

GOD CAN CLEANSE ANY SITUATION

God can clean up any lifestyle and make you new. Although God gives you the free will to choose the lifestyle you want to live on this earth, if you want to enter Heaven you have to make a change. Heaven is a Holy place and if you want to enter in, you have to turn from ungodly living to living Holy and righteous in the Lord.

Perhaps your lifestyle falls in one of the categories listed in 1 Corinthians 6:9-11 of sexual sin, worshipping idols, adultery, prostitution, homosexuality, thief, greedy, drunkard, abusive, cheater, and many other sins. None of these sins will enter the kingdom of God. Nevertheless, God loves you so much because He still gives you hope after warning you about sin, judgment, and destruction.

The Bible says that you can come out of these sinful strongholds by calling on the name of Jesus and by the power of the Holy Spirit. If someone says you will always be like you are or you can't be delivered, just remember these awesome words in 1 Corinthians 6:9-11: "And such were some of you: BUT ye are washed, but ye are sanctified, but ye are justified in the name of the Lord Jesus, and by the Spirit of our God." God purposely listed sin that we consider hardcore and major (although sin is sin) and then says some were like that but not anymore because God made you holy through Jesus. Hallelujah!

Although indulging in sin may feel good to the body and is a challenge to let go, you can overcome sin in the name of Jesus. I pray that you can make the initial steps to call on Jesus and desire in your heart to receive the Holy Spirit. I have never witnessed a person remain the same if they really let God touch them, consistently do the things that will make them stronger spiritually and stick with Him. You can be cleansed if you stay long enough with God to let Him make you over. God specializes in healing messed up situations. Do not lose hope.

It is so important to cry out to God and say Lord free me! Lord empty me of everything and fill me up with your Spirit. You can be washed from anything through Jesus and His Holy Spirit. But do not wait too late to get this process started. If we haven't let Him cleanse us by the time Jesus returns for the believers or before we leave this earth, then we will not enter the kingdom of Heaven. The spiritual cleansing process may not be easy, but it will be worth it to make a change in order to spend eternity with the Lord.

Sometimes it is hard for people to break free because of who they are connected to. You can progress better in the Lord when you make connection changes and break away from people who keep you in ungodly situations. Although it may be challenging and hurtful, sometimes you have to tell people that you need a break and a separation so that you can focus and get stronger. Separation is worth it so that you can draw closer to God and live in heaven with Him when you die.

Ask God to restore and renew you if you fall. In 2 Samuel 12, David was an anointed king and leader of God who lost his way. He took another man's wife, had her husband murdered, and had a baby with her. However, he lost the baby. And God said the sword wouldn't leave his lineage. But God blessed him with a new son, Solomon. The Bible says David washed, anointed, changed his apparel, and came to the house of the Lord to worship. God restored David and wants to do the same for you!

COME OUT OF YOUR SPIRITUAL CAVE

God is calling people who are hiding in spiritual caves to come out and do His will. Sometimes, warfare, trials, and fear can push you into a cave where you stop working for God. For example, some people stop serving God because of problems in the family, church, work, or personal life. There are times of rest. But God does not want His vessels to become comfortable in caves and abort their assignment. Do not allow anything to stop the work of God in your life. Let nothing separate you from the love of God (Romans 8:38-39).

In 1 Kings 19, the man of God, Elijah, experienced a spiritual cave. He worked hard for God and as a result received a death notice from Jezebel. Jezebel said she was going to kill him because God used him to let everyone see that her prophets and gods were false and he slew them. Elijah hid in a cave because of the death threat.

He became so comfortable in sleeping in the cave and pausing his work for God, God sent an angel to his cave to constantly wake him up and provide food so that he could eat and arise to do God's will. The Lord was not through with Elijah even though he was fearful and depressed because of his situation. God did not let him off the hook from his mission just because trouble was in his life.

God is so loving and awesome that He will come find you in your cave. He will send an angel, a servant/messenger of God, to refresh you, feed you with His manna and tell you to still go do your assignment even in the midst of everything that may not be going well. Spiritual threats, darts, and various adverse situations come at you when you're really working for God. But God will cover and encourage you to continue pressing towards the mark for the prize of the high calling in Christ Jesus (Philippians 3:14).

Trouble and trials do not give you a pass to abort the God-ordained missions and assignments in your life. God already has the plan to bring you out and turn it around. Thanks be to God who always causes us to triumph (2 Corinthians 2:14).

God loves us so much to check on us, strengthen us, and send people in our lives to help us press through during the rough times. God listened to what was bothering Elijah but afterward still told him to get out of the cave and go pray for and anoint people. God is not for anyone staying comfortable in a cave to avoid doing their calling regardless of how bad your situation is. We are commissioned to go share Jesus Christ with the world and "Be instant in season, out of season" (2 Timothy 4:2). In other words, always be ready to share the good news in every season even when you may not feel like it.

God wants you to always be about His business. He will comfort you along the way and get you through situations. Elijah experienced warfare, but His work wasn't finished because He had to go pray for the next king and anoint and prepare his successor, Elisha. Elijah had a very good reason to lay low because he did not want Jezebel to kill him.

God didn't take Elijah's valid reasons or excuses and He will not accept our excuses. God has already equipped us if we keep on the whole armor of God. Because Elijah came out of the cave and remained faithful to God, his enemy, Jezebel was killed and

Elijah wasn't touched. Elijah miraculously went to Heaven through a whirlwind.

I pray that you come out of every cave and do the work of God.

BE ROOTED IN GOD AND NOT PEOPLE

What happens to your walk with God if the people you admire spiritually decide to stop following God? What if a world spiritual leader who is valued decides to give up? What if the minister turns away from the gospel? Will you say well, if they stop then I know I can't make it either? If you love the Lord, it is hurtful to see others give up on God. Although it may be challenging, stay focused and free in God. Pray for people to return to God, but never stop serving God because of the decisions of others to stop.

You will give up easily if your salvation is only built upon people. God wants us to go beyond just hearing of Him. He wants us to have a personal, everlasting love relationship and know His Word for ourselves so that no matter what, we will be grounded in the sure foundation of Jesus Christ. Don't allow people to be your only source of spiritual survival.

It is encouraging to listen to the messages from God's servants, receive wisdom, and admire others. However, do not let any of it take the place of your personal relationship with God. Can you stand if all of it is stripped away? Can you pray and get a word from the Lord for yourself? Are you strong only in people or in the Lord? God wants us to be strong in Him and in the power of His might (Ephesians 6:10).

We should sharpen and encourage one another because it is helpful and beneficial to our walk and freedom in Christ. But don't let it be your only source of spiritual survival because what if they get tired of sharpening your iron? We should read the Word of God in addition to encouragement from others because it is the main source that sharpens our iron.

Don't rely on people to be your food that keeps you from dying of hunger spiritually. Let the encouragement from others be your added seasoning to what you are already eating from the master's table. The food that sustains you is Jesus and His Word because He is the Bread of Life. God wants you to dine and eat at His table with Him. If you want to eat with Him and want to be filled, spend time with Him. Read your Bible. Pray. If you hunger and thirst for righteousness you shall be filled (Matthew 5:6).

Do not just rely on others to be your spiritual life support because if they pull the plug, can you still breathe and live spiritually without them? Make sure your life support is up hooked to Jesus Christ so that you can still breathe, live, and press on in the Lord. Become stronger in the Lord so that you can stay with Him no matter how bad things get in the world, church, or around you. No matter what happens stay with Jesus. If you see others abandon God, don't give up on Him because

He will never ever give up on you. God says He will never leave us nor forsake us (Hebrews 13:5). Hallelujah.

I invite you to say this prayer: God, thank you for the people you have in our lives to encourage us in you. Jesus, we want to be able to stand even if we don't have anyone. God, please be our bread and water. The fountain of others can run out, but Jesus, you never run out and we can drink from your well freely. Lord help us to develop a true relationship with you. Reveal yourself in a real way so that we may know you personally. Teach us who you are. Make us strong in you. Speak to us in your word and give us understanding. Help our focus to stay on you even when we see things in the church or the lives of your people that aren't of you. Help us to pray for them and not follow in their sinful ways. Things are getting worse in the world so please give us that firm foundation built on the solid rock which is Jesus Christ. In Jesus' name, Amen.

3

ACTIONS MOVE GOD

"Seest thou how faith wrought with his works, and by works was faith made perfect?" -James 2:22

SHOW YOUR FAITH

Whatever you're asking the Lord for, put your foot on at least one step and go towards it. Show your faith. God is about action and movement. In the Bible, He tells people to "Go, Come, Get" and many other "action" words where they had to move towards the blessing.

God does not always give the entire plan beforehand, but He releases further instructions as you take each step. Use courage and faith to put your foot on the step even though you don't know the details ahead. Why should God pour out all of the instructions in our life and we aren't even going to move anyway and take a leap of faith to step #1?

Think about your prayer requests. Yes, you prayed, but what have you done to activate your faith and show action in that request? Many people are waiting on God to just drop stuff in their lap just because they prayed. But the key is to know that faith without works is dead (James 2:17). Work towards what you ask God for. Even when you pray for others, you can show action by planting seeds and words of God in their life. God is really about "us" moving and being obedient. If God says you must do something first, do it. Obedience in action is the way to receive answers to your prayer requests.

There are so many unanswered requests because sometimes all we do is ask, pray and just sit there year after year waiting and looking up. And God is looking at us waiting to see our faith towards what we asked for. It took me years to realize oh, if I desire something, I have to yes pray about it, but then give it 100% and pursue it because God does not move at all until He sees my faith in action. I have to do everything I can, plant seeds, inquire about it, and let God do the rest and wait on His full manifestation. You will feel so much better when you pursue what you pray for versus just sitting there. Don't just sit there anymore. Yes, wait on the Lord but make sure that in your waiting you did something to help your request manifest. Revisit some of those requests and you will see that God is just waiting on you to activate your faith (James 2:22).

Don't just ask God for requests, but seek and knock (Matthew 7:7). The hindrance to the manifestation is asking and waiting with no action. "Waiting on God" does not mean to just sit there in prayer and faith. God is waiting on us to yes ask, but then go seek and knock. God already has the table prepared (Psalm 23:5). Therefore, step out of your comfort zones to go receive, find, and walk in the doors that God will open for you. God releases blessings as we make moves to prepare for what we prayed for. Release your faith and at least make preparation.

God will move as your faith in action increases. Your faith is connected to you reading and hearing the word of God and believing it (Romans 10:17). Let your eyes read the word of God, let your ears hear it, let your spirit receive it and do your best to obey and live it. God is looking for the faith that is tied in with

His Word. Listen and watch sermons, read spiritual posts on social media, but don't forget to read God's word for yourself so that your faith can get stronger. God isn't going to move just because you follow, listen to, or attend the church of someone with great faith. Jesus repeatedly notes that requests are granted according to your faith (Mark 10:52, Matthew 9:29-30).

DO SOMETHING FOR GOD

God has deposited something on the inside of all of us where we can get involved to serve and use our gifts. Some may not know their gift. You can still serve or do something for the Lord until your gift is revealed. Pray and see where God leads you to get started. As you get started, your gifts will unfold and hopefully someone in your ministry or a connection can help you seek God to see what you're called to do. There is a plan and purpose for everyone. Matthew 25:21 says, "Well done thy good and faithful servant." A servant doesn't sit all the time. A servant is up and moving.

Deliverance and transformation happen more when you at least start trying to serve. God can deliver you while you're serving in action. God is touching you and working things out when you do services such as standing at the church door ushering, singing, helping in a ministry, out in the community with your church and many other areas. You do not have to be in a church building to serve. You can help a neighbor, care for the elderly and infirmed, and volunteer.

Some people wait until their life is totally cleaned up to start serving God and being active in ministry. But God starts moving when we start moving for Him. I learned that God never wants me to stop using my gifts because He is transforming my life and making me better as I stay on fire for Him. If we wait until we are totally transformed to do something for God, we'll be waiting forever and with no results. God wants to free you from the phrase and excuse that "I'm not doing anything for God because my life is messed up." As you start doing something, God will move in your life.

People become cold spiritually when they stop doing their gifts for God. You were born to do what God gifted you to do. Blessings flow, healings come, deliverance and the awesome transformation process takes place as we become active in God. Never stop doing the gifts God gave you.

The enemy loves Christians who don't do their gift. You are not a threat to the devil when you never get involved in your church ministry; you only sit on the pews, don't attend service, and never use your gifts in the kingdom of God. Our gift within is what blesses us individually and others spiritually as well as in many other ways. So if you aren't blessing anyone with your gifts, the enemy is happy. But don't let him win. Stir up your gifts (2 Timothy 1:6).

A lot of Christians forget that church attendance and listening to the word is awesome, but what about eventually doing something for God? That's where your blessing lies. Anybody can come to church and sit down. You can even do that home in your pajamas. But what about getting out of your comfort zone and begin to do something for God?

You will be amazed once you learn what God has given you. You have gifts that are sitting within you that need to be stirred up. One of the awesome things I love to experience is being around people who demonstrate their gifts from God! It blesses me and others so much. You will feel and know when you connect with someone who uses their gifts. You will be blessed indeed! Use your gifts in the kingdom of God and it will spread to all areas of your life. Somebody is waiting on your gifts right now.

SPEAK LIFE AND RESURRECT YOUR PURPOSE

It may seem silly to speak life to people, situations, problems, or anything dead, broken, failing, not coming together or not prospering. But never stop speaking life. You speak life by declaring God's living words and verses to it until you see change.

God's words are so powerful that they never return unto Him void, but they accomplish what pleases Him (Isaiah 55:11). It is a blessing that we can use God's words because sometimes we don't know what to say to our situations. Therefore, we can let God's word, who has all power, do the talking and moving.

Don't lose hope if it takes a "minute" to see things come to pass after you speak life. Some situations may take years to blossom. Even if you do not see any movement right away, continue to speak the Word of God because His words always produce something and eventually give life. It prospers and causes things to happen!

Sometimes God doesn't show us any progress or movement in situations we are praying for. It may get worse and just go in the opposite direction of what we want. But when God's Word, timing, and release happen, God will move in a special way in situations that we think will never become alive! In Ezekiel 37:10, Ezekiel prophesied and spoke to dead, dry bones and they became life and an army.

Do not allow people or situations to stop you from speaking life, resurrecting your purpose, and pursuing what's in your heart. Our purpose is already in us. It tugs at our hearts until we walk in it. Do not bury your purpose just because people may not believe. Whether they believe it or not, it will constantly be a weight or desire inside of you until you walk in it. We may try to get people or things to fulfill us. True fulfillment is when you pursue the things in your heart and walk in your God-given purpose.

Your purpose may seem small, dumb, useless, and just insignificant to others. Let it "appear" that way. Go after and do what you love. If you love what you do, what you produce will be effective and you will be fulfilled. Some people feel they have to go after the positions that are esteemed by the world so they can appear to be successful. What good is it just to appear successful and you don't even enjoy what you do? You may want to work at a job or start a business that is not "considered" to be hyped up by the world. Don't go with hype or appearance; go with your heart.

I believe true success and fulfillment is to explore and do the things you want. For example, if you enjoy cleaning, start a cleaning business. You will put your heart into cleaning because you love it. And as a result, you will make customers happy because of your work, and you will earn money doing something that does not really feel like a job to you. You never know how your business or purpose will grow into something big all because you followed your heart, spoke life, and resurrected your purpose.

4
USE YOUR KEYS

"And I will give unto thee the keys of the kingdom of heaven: and whatsoever thou shalt bind on earth shall be bound in heaven: and whatsoever thou shalt loose on earth shall be loosed in heaven."

-Matthew 16:19

THE WORD OF GOD IS THE KEY

You will live a defeated life if you do not keep the Word of God in your heart. The Word of God is the key. You will be victorious if you consistently read it and live by it. No, you don't have to read it every second of your life because that isn't possible. Just start out small by reading a verse before you begin your day. And then talk to God (pray). Daily devotionals that have a scripture is a really good start. You can use the tools of your choice. The point and goal are for you to read the Bible every day. And as you grow, you want to make time to study it too.

Reading, studying, and increasing your time in the Bible will really change you and your situation. I read the Bible a lot when I first got saved because I wanted to be free from the powerful ungodly strongholds in my life. If I was not dedicated, I would not have been in my right mind today. I would still be an unhappy, bound-up person that is faithful in going to church and serving, but my heart far from Christ.

It does not matter your title or how anointed and gifted you are, if you slack in your personal word time and prayer, you will get weak spiritually. If you proclaim to be saved, sanctified, and filled with the Holy Ghost, just imagine if you go weeks and months without reading the Bible. You will be surprised at the ungodly things you will find yourself doing or thinking. Nothing else will deliver you from the power of Satan, except the word of God. So please don't think you will be victorious in your Christian walk without consistent Bible reading. You will constantly live in defeat. But God wants you to be happy, free, and at peace on this journey with Him. The key is the Word of God.

The Word of God WILL make a difference in your life. Do not say the Bible or church doesn't work because you keep falling into sin. It is a personal decision to fulfill and act on the desires of your flesh. Satan makes sin so appealing that it can actually distract you from your God-given assignment.

I assure you that the Word of God is more powerful than any and everything. Hebrews 4:12 says, "For the word of God is alive and powerful. It is sharper than the sharpest two-edged sword, cutting between soul and spirit, between joint and marrow." It exposes our innermost thoughts and desires. You will NOT be defeated if you get into it, stay with it, pray it, learn it, and attend a Spirit-filled church led by a pastor after God's own heart.

You can pray all day, but God moves when He hears His Word. That's why there are so many unanswered prayers because you have to put the Word with it. You will then see more answered prayers. Apply a verse in the Bible to your situation or prayer request and God will honor His word if it's His will for your life.

USE THE POWER

Ephesians 3:20 says, "Now unto him that is able to do exceeding abundantly above all that we ask or think, according to the power that worketh in us." God is more than able to do what we ask or think. But sometimes we just are not working the power in us. You use the power by stirring up, communing with, making time for the Power of the Holy Ghost which is the Spirit of God. Stay connected and active with the power source of God's Word. Make time to read the Bible, listen, learn, receive, pray, talk to God, worship, fellowship with others in the Lord.

We have to be connected to God if we want Him to move in our life. Sometimes we can become distant from God, don't make time for Him, and then say God isn't answering prayer. God is still so merciful and loving that even when we are distant or not doing what He wants us to do, He still answers prayers!

One of my testimonies is that when I was in a sinful situation, just totally living in a way opposite of what pleases God years ago, He chose to still work a miracle in my life. It seems like He would have did it only when I was doing good and not in situations that didn't please him. But now I see He did it to show his love and that He does hear the prayers of sinners when we begin with repentance. He showed up in a powerful way that changed my life because I begin to pray and ask for help and ask God to change me while I was yet in the situation. God is so good indeed. My testimony is why I tell people no matter how ugly your situation is, God can transform you and your life.

God wants to answer every prayer and do even greater things in our life. But His movement is according to the power that works in us. It is important to pray, Lord work your power in me. Help me to be connected and not distant from you. If I have been distant, help me to reconnect and stay connected.

God can answer requests in our life in a second, do miracles and all kinds of awesome things in the blink of an eye without us having to do anything. However, most of the time God will not release some blessings until we line up with Him. Do not just line up to receive things from God. But line up to have a steadfast relationship with the Lord.

God is looking for vessels that are willing to be used by Him and who will allow Him to work His power through. There are many people that don't have time for God. But God is still looking for that remnant (small group) that He can work through because there is so much to be done in the Kingdom of God. It does not take a lot of people, like we may think, for God to move. He can use one or just a few people to impact millions and get them on track with His purpose.

Commit to becoming part of the remnant where we let God work His power in us to draw others to Christ. God can do amazing things in our life, but He wants to see if we are willing vessels that the Holy Spirit can work through to accomplish His will. We may constantly pray for different requests. He will answer more as we get in place so that He can use us. Be on fire for God and let the power work in you.

THE POWER OF PRAISING AND WORSHIPPING GOD

Your praise and worship are more powerful than you know. Every time you glorify God whether it is verbal words, singing, lifting your hands, in dance, and many other ways, something is shifting in you, in your atmosphere, and in your situations. Do not let a day go by without saying something to God -- Hallelujah, Thank You Jesus. Even if you don't give a request every day just say something to God in thanks. "Thank You Jesus" only takes a few seconds.

Learn to praise God even when you aren't in a church service. You don't need any music to say God I Thank You! Praise God in your own way. Some may feel like they "can't praise God" until they get back in the church building or church service. But oh no, there isn't a limited special time or way to praise God. Worship music is a blessing and helps you to worship the Lord even more. But whether you have music playing or not, you can always say thank you Lord!

Praise and worship cause God to turn things around. There are times for inward thanks. But be sure as much possible that you speak your praise out in the atmosphere and watch God begin to shift things in your life. God seeks true worshippers

(John 4:24). Therefore, if you want God close to you and want Him to answer your prayers, worship Him.

Keep on the garment of praise to keep off heaviness. When you don't wear or keep on the garment of praise, the spirit of heaviness will wear on you (Isaiah 61:3). God makes an exchange with us. Praise Him and He takes away our heaviness. If you never praise God or spend time telling Him thank you, you will feel a heaviness in your life. You may feel like you're drowning in your problems. That's because you aren't taking a break from everything else to praise the one who created you.

Praise encourages God to move on your behalf and do even more for you because it shows that you notice his goodness and awesomeness. It shows that you have your eyes on Him and believe in Him. We praise people, which is good and beneficial. But don't praise people or things more than God because people can't do what God can do. Praise the one who can fix your situation. Praise and Worship refreshes you and brings peace. It refreshes you because you are glorifying God. Anytime you glorify God, He will move on the inside of you for uplifting Him. Get the heaviness out of your life by praising God not just on Sundays or in church but do it daily because it truly blesses you.

As you worship, God is setting up the ambush against your enemy. 2 Chronicles 20:22 notes that when the people of Judah begin to sing and praise that the Lord sets ambushments against their enemies. When you enter a battle, set yourself to pray, seek and worship God. Do not let fear consume you because the Almighty God will fight for you if you let Him.

Even though you may want to go ahead and fight the battle your way, stand still in God's word. Sometimes it is hard to be still and silent because you don't want your enemy to think they're going to defeat you since they do not see any movement from you. Silence, being still, and holding your peace does not mean you are defeated. It means you are waiting on God to fight for you. As you wait...sing, worship and praise God. The ambushment is you hiding in God. As you continue to worship God in the battle, He will attack and destroy your enemy by surprise! The battle is not yours, it is the Lord's. Your praise and worship are powerful.

5

GOD IN THE FAMILY, HOME & RELATIONSHIPS

"As for me and my house, we will serve the LORD." -Joshua 24:15

THE BENEFITS OF CONNECTING WITH SPIRIT-FILLED PEOPLE

Attach yourself to people who are in love with God and Spirit-filled, not just churchgoers or people who profess to be saved and not live it. You will automatically feel the fruit of the Spirit (Galatians 5:22-23) of love, joy, peace, longsuffering, gentleness, goodness, faith, meekness, temperance and so much more from these connections.

Friendships, relationships, and marriages work better when the Spirit of God is in the center and flowing in them because then love, peace, and patience will be present. It will not be a struggle to radiate these positive vibes. You will not have to beg for loving qualities because it will flow from the person if they are truly Spirit-filled. Spirit-filled relationships are not perfect and will experience opposition at times. But the spirit of peace will work together to get things back on track.

Being around Spirit-filled people regardless of their age, race, or social status gives me joy, happiness, and empowers me because I experience the characteristics of God listed in Galatians 5:22-23. I purposely and closely attach myself to people who are in love with God and show it in their lifestyle and actions so that I can feel real love from them and not a lot of foolishness. I truly enjoy being around and talking to all people, even if they aren't spirit-filled because if we have God, He gives us love for everyone. But be careful and choose wisely who you have strong connections with.

Too much closeness and comfortability with someone who is not walking with God can rotten your godly fruits within. If you get too comfortable and develop close ties with ungodly spirits, then you could potentially begin to act like them because evil communication corrupts good manner (1 Corinthians 15:33). For example, if I constantly have a closeness with someone who gossips, I am more likely to participate and do the same because that's what I'm exposed to.

Your relationships and closeness with others determine what will come out of you. Therefore, choose wisely and with purpose. It is just something awesome and special when you have a closeness with people of the same heart and mind, especially in God. Even if you aren't saved, you will feel a positive vibe, energy, and uplifted on the inside when you connect with a true believer. That's why it is important to receive the Holy Spirit and ask God to fill and baptize you. The gifts and fruit of the Spirit are powerful, real, and undeniable because everyone can see or feel it, even if they do not want God. God will surround you with love and these beautiful characteristics when you do your best to love Him and know Him.

Staying yielded to the Spirit helps you not to carry out what the flesh wants. There is already a battle of flesh and spirit, so don't make it easy for the flesh to win by habitually staying in or making wrong connections. Go purposely make spirit-filled connections. If you connect with people who say they are Christians but don't live it, you will do the same. But go after spiritual connections, because the spirit will be victorious over everything!

Non-spirit-filled relationships keep you comfortable in doing wrong, but spirit, love-filled relationships convict you and help you to do right. I do not want anyone to tell me my sin is okay or not say anything because silence is just a quiet compromise.

Throughout life, my God-filled friendships and relationships have been peaceful, very fun, and have helped me to grow and fulfill my purpose. The times that I did not have these connections in my life is when I experienced the opposite of love, joy, and peace. That is because Christians need real spirit-filled connections to survive and stay strengthened.

God says it is not good for man to be alone. He wants us to stay connected with other true believers because two is better than one (Ecclesiastes 4:9). In the Bible, God had people to work with a partner or in groups. Jesus purposely went out and made 12 friends that he could fellowship with and who helped him to fulfill his purpose. He trained them and showed them how to do the will of God. Therefore, there is POWER in unity and agreeing relationships. A true friend, relationship, and helpmate pushes and encourages you to be and do better, not hinder or stop you.

The Spirit of God does not try to frustrate or discourage your purpose in God. If people do that, unfortunately, they are not walking in the Spirit because the Spirit doesn't fight the Spirit. The Spirit of God brings out the best in you and wants you to succeed and prosper in Jesus' name. Seek God-filled connections because when you're surrounded by real love, the love of God and His Spirit, you are definitely better off.

CONNECT WITH PEOPLE WHO HELP YOU FULFILL YOUR PURPOSE

Be in relationships, friendships, and marriages that help you fulfill your purpose. Walk in the will of God together. Purpose is not just trying to get rich, famous, and achieve your dreams. People who only strive for this can have everything but still leave this earth unhappy and with a void. If you only aim for high status as a couple, family, or individual without God, there will still be a void because we were created to worship God and walk in His plan for us. We are fulfilled when we walk in God's assignment for our life. I am not saying that you will never have disappointments in your life even after you're walking in His will, but you will be fulfilled knowing that you are doing what God called you to do.

Connecting with someone just because they have climbed the ladder and have a lot of material things clearly does not mean you will experience the same things, nor does it guarantee happiness. There are so many people that have nice cars, houses, high-paying jobs, and material things but their household is hell. They look happy on the outside to everyone else, but you never know what is actually going on behind closed doors especially where no one is pursuing God and his purpose. This also applies to households where one is pursuing God and the other is not. War, friction, and discord can occur because 2 Corinthians 6:14 notes, what communion have light with darkness? Some people still force these connections and put up with the war for various reasons. God does not force us to deal with the pain that comes from unequally yoked connections because He already tries to warn us not to do it in 2 Corinthians 6:14.

Problems arise in spiritual households too, but if God is really in both individuals, He will help those who keep Him in the center. The spirit of long-suffering, one of the fruits of the Spirit, will supernaturally arise. Therefore, yes you can achieve a worldly status that makes you look good to everyone else but without God, you aren't guaranteed to have peace, love, and true happiness inwardly.

LET THE CHILDREN COME TO GOD

All babies have a special assignment from the Lord. And believe it or not, Luke 1:13-16 shows that God is so powerful that He can begin working with a child in their mother's womb.

God desires for families to be in church, especially so children can have the opportunity to learn about Him.

It may be comfortable and relaxing for the parent to stay away from spiritual environments and not have prayer and Bible reading in the home, but if the child is called and chosen by the Lord, it is like they're missing their spiritual oxygen tank.

If you are a parent or guardian, regardless of your current status in the church, as a person of faith, I want to encourage you to provide your children with at least a foundational knowledge of God. As they mature, they will then be able to make their own decisions but without an initial spark, they will be left to their own devices. As scripture states, "Train up a child in the way he should go: and when he is old, he will not depart from it (Proverbs 22:6)."

We all have a calling because we have a role in the kingdom. How will your child develop their calling if they are not in that nurturing environment? It is up to the parents to make sure to keep the child progressing spiritually. Some parents may not know how to provide spiritual nourishment to the babe and can allow someone else to help in this area.

Many times, kids receive nurturing in many areas but lack spiritual nourishment with the Lord. God gave a commandment to John's parents to not allow their son to drink strong drink. This means that even though kids are exposed to a lot at an early age nowadays, it is so important to pray to see how God wants the child to be raised because everything is not for everybody.

It is sad to observe that many of God's chosen kids aren't consistently being taught about God's word. And if they have a special assignment from the Lord, but the parents don't know, understand, or make the effort to be in church and have spiritual growth activities in the home, most times the child will eventually go more towards rebellion, acting out, and all kinds of situations at an early age. They can go from sweet to sour, without a spiritual environment. On the other hand, if they observe their parents constantly start and stop their own spiritual development, that can hinder their view and motivation to live for God.

Children need spiritual covering and hands-on development with the Lord so that they can have peace. A lot of times if they don't have the covering, the enemy comes into their life strong. He is happy that he can torment kids who are called to be the Lord's vessel but are uncovered spiritually.

When parents break a child's spiritual connection to God, they open the doors for many negative things to arise. Some parents are cold towards God and do not want anything to do with Him. But how the parent feels about God does not change the fact that God has marked their child to serve Him.

The parent may be comfortable in their ways and choose not to make time for God and the things of Him, but sometimes what we don't see is the hidden gem that God really wants to bless and cover the child. Even if a parent changes their mind about the Lord, it still doesn't change the fact that God has ordained their child from the womb and has a special purpose for them. God will continue to encourage parents to do what Ephesians 6:4 says "And, ye fathers, provoke not your children to wrath: but bring them up in the nurture and admonition of the Lord."

It can be hard for parents to accept that sometimes God has someone else that can help develop the child spiritually which impacts all other areas. In the book of 1 Samuel, Samuel was a young child and God begin to deal with him early. Eli, the priest gave him his first spiritual lesson of how to respond to the Lord. That took a lot of sacrifice for Samuel's parents to let him grow up in the house of the Lord and allow another person to help him progress spiritually.

Sometimes parents may not understand, but when God has a special assignment for your son or daughter, He will make it known in some way. Look at how the child responds to the things of God. Sometimes the Lord will send someone in the family's life to verbally say the babe is called, and sometimes God will simply keep beckoning the parent to get in or return to church not only for their own good but more so for the child because He knows what they will become in Him. God desires for his chosen kids to be in a spiritual environment to develop them for their calling in life.

Some kids who are called start off very excited for the things of God, but without proper and consistent spiritual nourishment and access to God, they can shift to the total opposite of Godly characteristics such as strong rebellion, disobedience, and various behaviors that can become strongholds early on. This occurs because they need strong, tight, consistent covering spiritually so that their gifts and the fruit of the spirit like love, joy, and peace can radiate from their life.

For some, it is a sacrifice for parents to include God. But the sacrifice is worth it because some kids are called by the Lord and they need access to the things of God to make it. Parents who recognize the call in their child's life and help groom it or allow someone to help will be blessed. So it is important for the parent to at least try to plant the seed of God and let them learn about God. When they become an adult, it will be their choice if they stay with God. But at least the parent would have obeyed God by introducing the kid to things of God and encouraging them along the way.

The enemy is after kids, especially the ones who God wants to use. It seems like he comes harder for the kids of Christian parents because of the spiritual seed that was planted. The goal is always to stop the seed of God because if it grows, the kid will be a blessing spiritually for God and others. Follow Jesus' words in Mark 10:13-14 to let the little children come unto Him.

POWER COUPLE

I believe a true power couple has the power of God in the center of their marriage. According to the world, power couples usually have status, money, and influence. It is a blessing to have material things and riches. But a lot of times when things go sour, those things don't keep the relationship together. Those things weren't "powerful" enough to keep things fastened. People could have even spent millions or a year's salary on a wedding and stay together for only a few months. Then some divorced couples hate each other and become bitter.

Luke 1:5-8 shows Zacharias and Elizabeth as a true power couple. I see true love. Elizabeth was barren and couldn't have kids for a long time. But it didn't stop Zacharias from staying with her. And the blessing is they didn't stop serving God. They didn't pout and say well God hasn't answered our prayers so we aren't going to serve Him anymore. Or one went to church and served and the other one didn't. The verses say they both walked in the ordinances of God. That means they both had some God action in their life. They were old and still served God. Zacharias still went to the house of God and served, and God did not forget their faithfulness. They had to wait a long time, but God answered their prayer to give them a baby, John the Baptist who grew up to be a powerful tool for God. This is an example of a power couple.

Power couples stay together and serve God together until they are old and leave this earth. That takes power, endurance, and love. This Bible story is also a great prayer for married couples to pray to the Lord asking to stay together. May God give married couples the power to endure and remain glued together.

Divorce is prevalent and happens so quickly nowadays. I've observed many Christian marriages and even Christian celebrity couples lose their character and get off track spiritually when things didn't go well in the marriage.

May God heal situations and help other people to avoid this hurtful process. I pray for God to keep people together and keep couples happy, at peace, and prospering. May God bless the singles to marry the right people so it doesn't have to end so quickly in bitterness. God heal, fix, and keep couples together in Jesus' name. And whatever reasons that keep breaking up especially Christian couples be broken in Jesus' Name.

Sometimes marriages may not work out the first time due to various reasons. But may the good Lord bless those who desire to be married again in Jesus' name. This will help more people to be happy and at peace. If peace and happiness are disturbed, then it impacts people spiritually. If they aren't happy, then they won't serve God as they should. They will be grumpy, bitter, and burdened because of relationship issues. And as a result, some people will not have the peace and full push within to do

God's will. This doesn't apply to just relationship issues. Anytime we are going through things and don't keep pressing through and let it weigh on us, we will slow up with God. But God desires for everyone to be serving Him and happy. God wants to heal every area, even non-relationship areas.

Zacharias and Elizabeth's godly marriage gives hope that you can be a power couple with the power of God in the center. You can serve God and stay together until the end of the earth.

6

EMPOWERED CHURCHES & LEADERS

"But ye shall receive power, after that the Holy Ghost is come upon you." -Acts 1:8

PULPIT ACCOUNTABILITY: TOOLS TO KEEP PASTORS FROM FALLING SPIRITUALLY

Sometimes church leaders fall because they fail to connect with someone that will truly hold them accountable. They may not develop a strong spiritual relationship with someone who can minister to them. It is important for church leaders and especially pastors to have at least one accountability partner.

Accountability partners who help spiritual leaders should possess various characteristics. They should be saved and filled with the Holy Spirit, rightly divide the word of truth, be trustworthy, have holy boldness, do not compromise with their leader, be prayerful, faithful to God, and honest.

Accountability partners will encourage, strengthen, and help maintain the spiritual wellbeing of the leader. Partnerships should include prayer, fasting, sharing of the word, truth, openness, and providing counseling to the leader.

When leaders feel they are failing or are about to be in error, they should communicate with the partner immediately. Accountability partners will follow up with the leader to see how they are coming along and have real talks. Leaders should be humble and willing to listen and accept correction. Leaders should lay down their pride, shame, and embarrassment and share with their accountability partner what they're really confronted with.

Overseers and leaders of God's flock should be blameless, have good behavior and integrity (1 Timothy 3:2). This is not to say they are perfect and will not sin or make mistakes. All have sinned and come short of the glory of God (Romans 3:23). God is merciful and forgives, but a leader of God should not habitually live in sin and simultaneously operate in the leadership position/calling. This double lifestyle causes a reproach to God's name and can wound God's people, especially Christians, but also the unsaved too.

Sometimes leaders and pastors should take a break from the leadership position until they are delivered so they can walk in integrity. Sometimes leaders can become tangled up in stronghold situations that are hard to overcome right away. Therefore, it is important for churches and ministries to develop strong, anointed leadership teams so that at any time if the leader is unable to minister due to sinful situations or other reasons, someone on the team can continue to feed the flock. Teams should be able to meet with leaders to discuss ungodly, uncomfortable situations and develop a plan to keep or get the church healthy again. It is not healthy for churches to know ungodly situations and not address it and allow the leader to bring reproach to God by not stepping down as they sort out their troubles. Matthew 18:15-17 says, "When your brother trespass against you, go and talk and include witnesses if need be."

Spiritual leaders need armor-bearers who will be in tune with their spiritual needs first and foremost. Some armor-bearers help their leaders by providing money and meals, making sure they look good physically, accompanying them, doing administrative work for them, and many other tasks. All of those duties are good and meet the pastor's physical needs. Unfortunately, sometimes a pastor can be surrounded by many armor-bearers who do all of this for them and they still fall spiritually. It is because their physical needs are met, but what about their spiritual needs? What about those issues they're dealing with secretly? Do they have someone they can talk to, get prayer, and have accountability?

It is important to make sure that pastors have accountability partners so their chances of falling spiritually will be decreased. Cover your pastor in prayer, the word of God, and fasting. Help be the "Iron that sharpeneth Iron"(Proverbs 27:17). Encourage them by speaking the word back into their life. Their spiritual soul needs to be fed too. Their spiritual battle is greater because God is using them to feed us and the enemy wants to "steal, kill, and destroy" (John 10:10). Sometimes leaders want to appear strong at all times. Don't let the "superman or superwoman" appearance fool you. They have struggles, tests, trials, hurts, disappointments and are tempted with sin too, but they don't have to be defeated because the accountability partner can uphold their leader's hand when they are weak and help them be victorious just like Aaron and Hur did for Moses (Exodus 17:12).

GOD IS EXPOSING THE SINFUL LIFESTYLES OF CHRISTIAN LEADERS

The reason why the world has and still is seeing so many church leaders (pastors, singers, musicians, and anyone who speaks God's word or represents him) sinful lifestyles exposed is because for one, God loves the person and wants them to repent and get it right. But also because God loves His people and He wants them free and not deceived no matter how great of a platform a person has.

If leaders fail to stay in the presence of God outside of using their gifts to serve the people, they can get caught up and begin to engage in all kinds of sin. The more leaders continue to sin and still continue coming before His people without a repentant heart, the more God will reveal so everyone can see. Leaders are better off not operating in their gift or leadership position until God delivers them and they are ready to be real with God. You can't really be used effectively by God when you live a habitual life of sin. If people continue to cover up and come in the house of God and serve like nothing is wrong, God will eventually expose you if He hasn't already.

When God exposes you, it is much more painful and affects so many people. That's why the Lord gives people time to confess to Him and stop doing what's displeasing in His eyesight. But if you continue, no matter how great your name is and anointed you are, rather now or years later, God will eventually show others if your private life truly matches your talk. The Lord wants you to really deal with your sin, repent, ask people for forgiveness, replace pride with humility, and receive healing so that He can use you for the kingdom.

David was a man of God who fell spiritually. In 2 Samuel Chapter 12, the prophet Nathan told David that he sinned in secret, but God was going to uncover it before everyone in Israel. David had to pay a price for his sin by losing the baby that came forth from his adulterous situation. Therefore, do not be deceived. God cannot be mocked. People will reap what they sow (Galatians 6:7). God will allow leaders to be mocked and embarrassed when they aren't sincere, but not His name and His Word.

Pray especially for the leaders of God because the enemy wants to embarrass them with the goal to mock the church so people can say why go to church? Some people are quick to say why go to church when the pastor is sinning like me or getting caught in scandals and in the news with ungodly situations.

Leaders are human and may fall too. But the key is when you fall, don't stay down in sin. Talk to God. Surround yourself with real Christians so you can cover each other in prayer.

Get back up and do the Will of the Lord. Remember that God can reveal when you continue to habitually live a secretive sinful life and try to lead people with no plan to make a change.

Leaders have to repent, too, and be honest with God behind closed doors so that they can go to heaven when they die.

Being a good leader and being successful with using gifts is not a guaranteed ticket to heaven. Leaders have to live holy and true even when they are not ministering. If leaders continue to play with the Lord and not live right when they aren't in front of others, they risk the chance of hearing the Lord saying depart from me ye that work iniquity (Matthew 7:23). But I pray that leaders will stay or get back on the straight and narrow way so that they can hear, well done thy good and faithful servant (Matthew 25:21).

SPIRITUAL GIFTS IN THE CHURCH

It is so important for ministers to know the gifts inside their ministry. The leader may have multiple gifts but may not have the gift of healing and/or miracles. Unfortunately, some leaders try to operate in every gift, even if they don't have them because they feel compelled to do so as the pastor. They don't seek out those who have it and let them use it. If you don't use the people and their gifts, then there will be lack and no change. It is also important for the members to participate in the ministries within their church so that their gifts can be recognized, nurtured, and developed.

Every person in the ministry is important from the child to the senior. Ephesians 4:16 says the whole body is fitly joined together…for the increase of the body unto the edifying of itself in love. Everyone has something in them that is a blessing to the body of Christ. It may be a little, quiet member sitting in the back who is faithful to God, praying behind the scenes that has the gift of healing. But if the leader doesn't recognize it or recognizes it but doesn't allow others to flow in their gift, then healing will be stifled.

Leaders hinder the flow of God if they monopolize spiritual gifts and only let the favorites in the ministry flow. The favorites may not have a spiritual gift that is ultimately blessing the body of Christ. That's why things aren't happening because all the gifts aren't in operation. The person with a gift that can help many may not have a title or position and that's where we mess up. The gifts can sometimes be stronger in people who do not have a title or position. And then these people and their gifts are overlooked because some ministries do not allow people to use their gifts if they do not have a title or position.

Some leaders are intimidated or afraid to let others use their gift, but it shouldn't be that way. The leadership calling isn't about us; it is about God's people. God's true and called leaders will get everyone involved because they know it isn't about them.

CARE ABOUT SOULS AND NOT MONEY

1 Peter 5:2 says, "To feed the flock of God which is among you, taking the oversight thereof, not by constraint, but willingly; not for filthy lucre, but of a ready mind." Churches and Leaders should let people know they care about them and not money. Regardless of the size of your ministry, create spiritually focused teams that will be hands-on with people and help them to grow.

More teaching emphasis should be put on the issues they're facing and deliverance versus giving and prosperity. People will give freely and abundantly if they see you care about them and you're doing right with God's money. Show people that you are using church funds to help others in need and furthering the gospel. Meet the needs of people in your own ministry. The Apostles did it (Acts 4:34-35). They did not use the money to live lavishly while their own people and community suffered. Reach out to the community, but don't let your own members be at home starving.

People in ministry should be blessed. Just be careful not to abuse God's money and pressure people for it. If you have integrity and your focus is on their soul and not gain, people will not mind blessing you. It will flow if you do not beg and demand. Speak messages that change lives for the better and they will continue to follow and bless the ministry. If you become a mega-pastor or millionaire righteously for changing lives, you deserve it. It is ok to live lavishly if God brought you to it and you did not exploit people. But remain humble, don't forget about His people, the needs, and the true purpose of ministry. Don't do outreach if you haven't even looked inward to try and help the struggling people in your church first. Do like the apostles in the Bible and distribute it.

If you really do not care for God's people and you're only in ministry for profit, please change your profession. Reconsider being a Spiritual Leader if you are only in it to generate money. Start businesses if you want money, but don't use the church and God's people to fill your pockets. Perhaps you need to work and also do ministry so that you can have finances. Not everyone can do the full-time ministry.

Don't set up a lot of engagements, programs, and church events to just make money. Events should be soul-focused. And yes, still have offering time. But preach and do so because you love God, want souls saved, and would be willing to do it for free. Can you still preach, give prophetic words, or use your gift if no one ever blesses you with an offering? If you have that attitude God will do the blessing and yes, use people to bless you.

Build and do things you can afford. Don't try to build extravagance just to keep up with church competition. Stay within your means and then you will not have to beg or be stressed financially with the house of God. Be content even if you have a small ministry. Your small ministry could be very effective and truly God-ordained. So do not be discouraged if you aren't big and or have a large membership. Ministry numbers don't always mean lives are being transformed. Just do your best to change lives and know that's very extravagant to God.

Read 2 Peter 2:3 to see how God feels about people who use His name to exploit people for money.

7
ARE YOU SAVED?

COME BACK TO JESUS

You don't have to be in a church building to receive God in your heart. Some may not make it to a building or to the altar. If something happens at this moment, are you confident that you're saved and will go with God when your time is up on this earth? If you are unsure, wavering, been on a God break, it is time to come back while you have the opportunity. Maybe you're a lukewarm person that wants to deal with God sometimes and other times you leave Him completely out. He doesn't want to have a little space in your heart where 90% of your life is with the enemy, distracted, or on worldly things, and 10% God. He wants all of you.

If you haven't totally surrendered and you're comfortable with being a part-time Christian, God wants us to choose this day who we are going to serve. God loves you and hopes you choose Him. You can receive God's salvation wherever you are. Say your prayer out to the Lord. Confess and believe in Jesus. Romans 10:8-10 says "But what saith it? The word is nigh thee, even in thy mouth, and in thy heart: that is, the word of faith, which we preach; That if thou shalt confess with thy mouth the Lord Jesus, and shalt believe in thine heart that God hath raised him from the dead, thou shalt be saved. For with the heart man believeth unto righteousness; and with the mouth confession is made unto salvation." After you do this, please find a good Bible teaching church where you can grow spiritually and get stronger.

Connect with a spiritual mentor to check on you, pray with you, and hold you accountable. Don't be ashamed to connect or reach out for spiritual help. You can do it! God's got you. Get ready for a journey of change and transformation. Don't give up! Keep pressing. It is your time. You and God.

DON'T MISS IT

Don't miss your opportunity to truly receive the gift of salvation. Not everyone will have a chance to cry out to God and make a change during the last moments of their life. You may not have the time or seconds to think, pray, or open your mouth to confess to the Lord.

To receive the gift of salvation, confess with your mouth that Jesus is Lord and believe in your heart that God raised him from the dead (Romans 10:9). Many do believe and quickly say "I'm saved!" But keep in mind that even devils believe (James 2:19-20). Therefore, turn your belief into action by living a life of repentance.

Many believe but still do not have the Holy Ghost, which is the power of God. They do not have the Holy Ghost because they haven't repented and been baptized. Repent means to turn away from sin and to feel such regret for past conduct as to change one's mind regarding it.

Acts 2:38 says, "Then Peter said unto them, Repent, and be baptized every one of you in the name of Jesus Christ for the remission of sins, and ye shall receive the gift of the Holy Ghost." The Holy Ghost comes into the vessel that's ready to receive and ready to live "Holy". We have to follow holiness in order to make it into heaven and see the Lord (Hebrews 12:14).

Your life should show fruit you have truly repented and turned away from your old self to become a new creature in Christ (Matthew 3:8). If you have truly confessed and believed, when are you going to walk in your newness? When you stop playing around and wholeheartedly get in Christ, there will be a new you. All things will become new (2 Corinthians 5:17). In order to become a new person in Christ, you have to first truly desire it in your heart. And then you should put consistent action into following God. You can't just give up after a week, month, or year. You press, sacrifice, and work out your salvation until the end. You have to endure in your spiritual walk until the end (Matthew 24:13). Have you been baptized? Acts 2:38 says to repent and be baptized. Even Jesus was baptized (Matthew 3:16). Water baptism is very important. Many get baptized when they're young or just to do it. But oh, what a great day it is when you decide to repent and be baptized with understanding because you are sincere and ready to "work out your salvation".

Please do not be deceived. Many believe and say they are saved. But in order to get into heaven, you have to make a change by repenting and continuing to follow Jesus in your life. Even people who believe and do good works in the church will not make it into heaven if they do not repent and turn away from the ways that aren't of God. Matthew 7:21-23 shows that if you are in church already, you believe or may even have a title/leadership position, if you play around with God and just do the outward acts in church but live a total opposite life that is not of God, you will not make it in if you do not repent. Do not miss your opportunity of salvation and repentance. Being saved is a blessing. Remember that everything on this earth is going to pass away. There is going to be a new heaven and earth one day!! (Isaiah 65:17, 2 Peter 3:13, Revelation 21:1) So make sure to be saved and do your best to live for the Lord.

Some people are truly ready to be set free and allow God to work in their life, but they do not know where to start. They can attend a church, but if they don't have anyone working with them on a personal level, they can still feel lost, bound, and don't know how to keep growing.

After you repent and accept Christ in your heart, ask Him to fill you with His Spirit. Never stop asking God to fill you (even for those who have been saved for years.) His Spirit is what really breaks the chains in your life. It is a process though, so don't get frustrated if you don't see immediate change.

Be persistent in prayer, asking for the Holy Ghost, and reading your Bible and God will begin to change you. Be in a church where you can grow and someone can work with you. It is hard to stay focused alone. Don't get lost in the crowd. Pair up with someone that can hold you accountable and pray for and push you. God desires to pour out His spirit on everyone (Joel 2:28). But not everyone will receive it if they are running from God. If you want God, He promises to fill you (John 14, 15, and 16).

ACKNOWLEDGMENTS

Glory to God forever. I love and thank the Lord for His help and blessing me to write this book.

I am thankful for my wonderful parents, Dad, William (Bill) Montgomery and Darling Mom, Overseer Annie B. Fields. I thank God for my Mom raising and instructing me in the Lord and showing me how to be a teacher and servant leader. I cherish every life lesson and encouragement from my Dad to always trust God and believe. My beautiful parents have supported and believed in every endeavor I pursued. Love and thanks to my Brother, Doric Montgomery, Sr. and nephew Doric, Jr. for supporting me and cheering me on.

Special love and appreciation to my Aunt, Pastor, and Mentor, Pastor Joyce Z. Freeman, Uncle, Deacon David Freeman and our church ministry, In the Name of Jesus Outreach Ministry. Aunt Joyce encouraged me to never stop writing for the Lord. Thank you for your prayers, encouragement, support, and helping me to walk in my calling.

Love and blessings to my family, cousin Pastor Chanda Jones and Family, Stepmom Margie and Family, Dr. Simi Adigun,

Aunt Jessie Myrick, mentors, friends, co-workers, students, Courageous Inspirations Family, and everyone who has believed in and inspired me.

Special thanks and blessing to my writing coach and editor, Mrs. Jackie "JC" Gardner for helping me to complete this project.

MY PRAYER FOR YOU

I hope this spiritual growth book has been a blessing to you. I pray that you will use your keys to live a successful life in Jesus. Always remember that God has already given you the keys to the kingdom of heaven (Matthew 16:19).

Heavenly Father,

Please touch the person holding this book in a special way. I pray that their life will never be the same. Empower them to finish the work you have started in them. Philippians 1:6 shows that you have started a good work in them, and you will perform it until the day of Jesus Christ. Thank you Jesus that they will be courageous and do your will with holy boldness. Thank you God for allowing your perfect love to cast out fear in their life. They are victorious and a powerful vessel in you. God, please heal, deliver, revive, set free and fill them with the abundance of your Holy Spirit. In Jesus' name, Amen.

ABOUT DOYVON MONTGOMERY

Doyvon (Dee) Montgomery lives in Jacksonville, Florida. She is an Evangelist, Educator, Business Owner, Singer, and Musician. Doyvon obtained her bachelor's degree in Sociology from the University of North Florida. She worked for various youth programs and started a tutoring business.

Her passion for teaching, mentoring, and working with youth led to her current career in Education. She has over 10 years of experience tutoring and teaching 6th-12th grade Math at private Christian, charter, and public schools.

Doyvon is the CEO and founder of Courageous Inspirations, a company that sells custom products and Christian apparel. Through Courageous Inspirations, she also enjoys sharing spiritual inspiration through blogs, podcasts, and songs. Her first song, "Hello Courage Goodbye Fear" was released in June 2021 and is available on all digital outlets.

Learn more about Doyvon at:

www.courageousinspirations.com.